CONT

Map references are denoted in the text by ❶ San Francisco & Golden Gate
Park ❷ Downtown ❸ Fisherman's Wharf ❹ Day Trips ❺ Public Transit

san francisco places to see

With its soaring hills and jaw-dropping views, wild ocean coastline and moody meteorological effects, San Francisco is hard to take for granted. Shimmering mists, sudden interplays of light, and swirling fogs transfigure the city on a minute-to-minute basis in a way that makes even its inhabitants catch their breaths. For exhilaration and free-thinking, few cities come close to San Francisco. Covering 49 square miles (127 sq km), it's a small, compact, and energetic place, divided into discrete neighborhoods that are crammed with coffeehouses, bars, and places to eat, and pulsating with theaters, galleries and music.

see it places to see

see it

Sights & Hoods

Alcatraz ❹

It's a five-minute ride by ferry to 'The Rock', the dour maximum-security prison where America's most infamous public enemies – including Al Capone, and Robert 'Birdman' Stroud – were incarcerated from 1934 to 1963 (the prison was closed after it was found to be cheaper to keep inmates at the Waldorf Hotel). For an extra $4.50, take the highly recommended audio tour, with its graphic descriptions of life inside the cellhouse, where prisoners were confined for up to 23 hours a day. SF's most captivating tourist attraction is also likely to be its

The island of Alcatraz with its isolated prison

coldest – book a week in advance and bring a sweater. Blue & Gold Fleet Bay ferries: _depart daily 9.30am-4.15pm (summer), 9.30am-2.15pm (fall, winter & spring), Pier 41 (❶ 1E). After-dark tours 7pm Thu-Sun, T: 415 705 5555, www.nps.gov/alcatraz_

Asian Art Museum ❷ 7C

This mammoth collection of Asian art (the largest outside Asia) moved in 2003 to sleek new headquarters in the Civic Center. Designed by Gae Aulenti – the architect behind the Musée d'Orsay station conversion in Paris – the museum fills a 1917 Beaux Arts building (the former San Francisco Public Library) with sky-lit galleries and a selection from a treasure trove of 14,000 objects spanning 6,000 years of stunning Oriental art. _Adm. Open 10am-5pm Tue-Sun, 10am-9pm Thu. 200 Larkin St at Fulton, T: 415 581 3500, www.asianart.org_

Cable Cars

People laughed at 'Hallidie's folly' but cable cars transformed the face

Cable car clambering up the hill

of San Francisco, making its steepest hills accessible and sparking off a real-estate boom. Scots-born Andrew Hallidie manufactured the wire-rope used in mines for hoisting ore along railway tracks, and cable cars work on similar lines, gripping a thick steel cable turned by a giant wheel at 9.5 mph (15 km/h). At their peak, 600 cars rattled through the city over 110 miles (177 km) of track: three lines are now in operation, with rides 'halfway to the stars' costing $5.00 (_see p.49_). See the

Cable Car Barn & Powerhouse (**2** 4D). *Open 10am-6pm daily Apr-Sep, 10am-5pm daily Oct-Mar. 1201 Mason St at Washington, T: 415 474 1887, www.sfcablecar.com*

California Academy of Sciences **2** 7E

Closed for a five-year renovation until 2008, some of the Academy's 14 million exhibits and the Aquarium can now be seen at 875 Howard Street. They cover every aspect of the earth, ocean and space. Thrills include a simulated earthquake ride, planetarium, and the Steinhart Aquarium, with its penguins, alligators, and 100,000-gallon Fish Roundabout. *Adm. Free 1st Wed of month. Open 10am-5pm daily, 10am-9pm Thu. 875 Howard St at 5th St in SoMA, T: 415 321 8000, www.calacademy.org*

California Palace of the Legion of Honor **1** 3A

This sublime collection covers 4,000 years of European art in a neo-classical building on a windswept clifftop looming over Golden Gate Bridge. Donated to the city by Alma Spreckels, the art-loving wife of a sugar magnate, the museum's star treasures include an original casting of *The Thinker* (one of 70 Rodins), furniture, porcelain, prints by Gauguin, and paintings by Seurat and Rembrandt. *Adm. Open 9.30am-5pm Tue-Sun. 100 34th Ave at Clement, Lincoln Pk, T: 415 863 3330, www.thinker.org/legion*

The Castro **1** 4E-4F

Castro is the exuberant hub of gay San Francisco, a place to stroll and primp and hang out; a shopping, bar, and restaurant mecca. On the

The rainbow flag welcoming you to Castro

corner of Market and Castro a giant 20 x 30-ft (6 x 9-m) rainbow flag flaps over Harvey Milk Plaza, commemorating the gay-rights activist assassinated in 1978. Close by is the Names Project, a 45,000-piece quilt memorial to AIDS victims, and a block away is the magnificent Castro Theatre (*see p.29*), an atmospheric 1922 movie palace still in pristine condition.

San Francisco's Free Sights

SF's free attractions include Golden Gate Bridge (*see p.8*), the Cable Car Museum (*see left*), the Museum of the City of SF (**1** 3E), the Fire Museum (**1** 3F), and the Maritime Museum (*see p.7*). Museums with free days are SFMoMA (1st Tuesday monthly, half-price Thursday eve, *see p.12*), the Academy of Sciences (*see left*), the Exploratorium (*see p.11*), and the Legion of Honor (free every Tuesday, *see left*). For other free events in the city, see www.sfarts.org

Tien Hau Temple in Chinatown

Chinatown ❷ 4E-5E

Dating from 1848 and settled by the laborers who were employed to build the transcontinental railroad in 1869, this is the oldest Chinatown in the US. A colorful mix of neon signs and dragon lamps, pagoda roofs and painted balconies, it's SF's most densely packed and bustling enclave, with people packed in like canned fish, and giftshops, dim sum parlors, temples, medicine stores, stalls, and markets scrambling for space. Eat moon cakes and lotus balls on the hoof, buy vintage silk and Ten Ren tea on Grant Ave (*see p.22*), watch fortune cookies being made at 56 Ross Alley, or pay your respects at 125 Tien Hau Temple (*125 Waverly Place at Clay*), which is dedicated to sailors, prostitutes, and writers.

Coit Tower ❷ 3E

For fabulous 360° views, take the elevator up 284-ft (86.5-m) Coit Tower, shaped like a fireman's hose and built with funds donated to the city by Lillie Coit, a much-loved eccentric and devotee of firefighters. Don't miss the lower-level WPA murals, painted by pupils of the Marxist artist Diego Rivera in 1934 (and so contentious then that a hammer and sickle were painted out). To the east of Coit, Filbert Steps drop down at 31.5° to Levi Strauss Plaza,

Fortune Cookies

'Chinese' fortune cookies are actually a San Francisco invention: Makoto Hagiwara, designer of Golden Gate Park's Japanese Tea Garden (❶ 5F), is credited with introducing them at the 1915 Panama-Pacific Exhibition; the first mass-produced cookies were made at the Hong Kong Noodle Factory in the 1920s.

the company HQ for the jeans invented by Levi Strauss in 1853, made of cloth from Nîmes ('de Nîmes') and resembling the pants worn by sailors from Genoa. *Open 10am-5pm daily. T: 415 362 0808, www.coittower.org*

Coit Tower was built in 1933

Paddle steamer at Fisherman's Wharf

Fisherman's Wharf ❷ 2D/ ❸

As well as shopping malls, waterfront seafood restaurants and a small army of sidewalk entertainers, SF's huge and touristy maritime theme park includes a fleet of vintage sailing ships, a 400-ft (122-metre) tunnel-aquarium, a World War II submarine (the USS *Pampanito*), and cheesy seafront diversions such as Ripley's

Believe It or Not! and the Wax Museum. The best attractions are less commercialized: sitting out on a cool day with a bread-bowl full of steaming-hot clam chowder; watching the sea lions (who migrated to Pier 39 after the 1989 Loma Prieta earthquake); and enjoying the free Maritime Museum, a whimsical 1930s Art Deco replica of a cruise liner. *Adm. Open daily. T: 415 561 6662, www.maritime.org*

SF CityPass

Good for nine days, SF City Pass gets 50% reductions to a grab-bag of attractions including SFMoMA, the Exploratorium, the California Academy of Sciences, the Palace of the Legion of Honor, and Blue & Gold Fleet Bay Cruise. The pass includes seven days of unlimited travel on Muni's cable cars, streetcars, and buses – buy it for $49 from sights or *www.citypass.net*

Golden Gate Bridge ❶ 1C

An architectural and engineering feat, an icon of the city and a joy to behold: San Francisco's wonder bridge took four years to build; its cables are long enough to wrap three times around the Earth, and in strong winds its deck can sway 27 ft (8 m) in all directions. On a clear, sunny day, take the 76 bus to the Toll Plaza and walk the 1.7 miles (2.75 km) across, or cycle and return by the Sausalito ferry (*see p.53*). www.goldengatebridge.com

The elegant spans of the Golden Gate Bridge

Golden Gate Park ❶ 4A-4D & 5A-6H

Sculpted out of wild and windswept duneland, Golden Gate Park is a 5-km (3-mile) slice of heaven stretching from Haight (*see p.9*) to the edge of the Pacific Ocean. The lush, exotic grounds take in a million trees, a herd of hairy bison (❶ 5B), a Japanese Tea Garden with Buddha and bonsai trees (❶ 5F), a restaurant with wonderful 1936 murals (the Beach Chalet, ❶ 5A), 75 acres of botanical garden (❶ 6F), and the California Academy of Sciences (*see p.5*). Explore on foot, by horseback (*see p.35*), or go pedal-boating with the turtles on Stow Lake (❶ 6E). Sundays – when the eucalyptus-scented grounds of the park are closed to traffic – are best for bikes and roller-blading. *Open dawn-dusk daily. Beach*

The Parrots of Telegraph Hill (❶3E)

When walking down Filbert Steps (*see box, p.13*), don't be surprised if you meet parrots. SF has two resident flocks: canary wings came in the 1970s (they are mentioned in Maupin's *Tales of the City*). In the 1990s, bigger, tougher red-masked parakeets muscled in and booted out the canary wings to less chi-chi quarters in the Mission. Existing on buds, blossoms, and berries, the rivals are the subject of an upcoming book and film as well as a host of urban myths.

Colorful shopping street in Haight-Ashbury

Chalet: T: 415 386 8439,
www.beachchalet.com

Haas-Lilienthal House ❷ 4B

Built for $18,000 in 1886, the sumptuous Haas-Lilienthal residence comprises 24 rooms and seven bathrooms, including a bidet, shower, and special gas-fired gadget for warming curlers. With its filigree trim and Tiffany glass, the Victorian house was custom-built for William Haas, a Bavarian who emigrated to America in 1865 and worked his way up from a grocer to become a director of the Wells Fargo Bank. Today it's the only private residence on beyond-exclusive Pacific Heights open to the public. For a frisson of 21st-century splendor, walk by the former Spreckels Mansion (❷ 4B), owned by author Danielle Steel, with 26 bathrooms and filling a whole city block. *Tours 12pm-3pm Wed, 12 noon-3pm Sat, 11am-4pm Sun. 2007 Franklin St, T: 415 441 3000, www.sfheritage.org*

Haight-Ashbury ❶ 4D-4E

Wannabe hippies, dreadlocked teens, spaced-out oddballs, and 60s nostalgics all eventually find their slightly stoned way to Haight-Ashbury. Four decades on from Flower Power, the delirious Haight has become a living symbol of '67 and the Summer of Love: walk up and down the main drag, Haight Street, and you'll be tumbled in a sea of psychedelia, from kids selling cheap weed and tattoos, bongs, and vintage clothing, patchouli, incense, tie-dye, and granola. Sacred holy grails include Hippie Hill, the Panhandle, and digs belonging to

The Crookedest Street

Some 750,000 cars a year wait in line to make the 5-mph (8-km/h) descent down Lombard St (❷ 3C), with its nine hairpin bends and the hair-raising gradient of 27 per cent. SF's twistiest street, meanwhile, is over on Potrero Hill on the 800-900 block of Vermont St bet 20th & 21st Sts (❶ 4H).

Startling ethnic murals in the Mission

hippie icons The Grateful Dead (*710 Ashbury*), Janis Joplin (*112 Lyon*), and Jefferson Airplane (*2400 Fulton*).

The Mission ❶ 4F

SF's colorful bohemian-Latino hood is also its warmest and sunniest, set in a valley with Twin Peaks to shield it from fogs. Settled by Spanish missionaries in 1776, and Mexicans and Latinos in the 20th century, it's now the place where San Franciscans like to eat, drink, and make merry; a vibrant mix of street art, bars, bodegas, and boutiques, plus some of the city's most happening restaurants, taquerías, and clubs. By day visit the Mission Dolores, built from three-foot-thick adobe walls in 1791, or take a guided tour of the famous murals adorning shops, schools, garage doors, and every inch of space available.
Mural tours: Precita Eyes, 2981 24th St at Harrison, T: 415 285 2287, www.precitaeyes.org

North Beach ❷ 3E-3F

Mellow and sun-dappled, Italian North Beach is the epicenter of neighborhood SF – the part that everyone likes best, the perfect trattoria, coffeehouse, and bookstore combination. Rents have spiraled and upscale boutiques have sprouted up but its bohemian heart beats on.

Top Views

With 43 hills, San Francisco has the best views – fog permitting (*see p.51*) – in the world. Viewpoints include sunset at Ocean Beach (as seen from Sutro Heights Park) (see above, ❶ 3A), or Cliff House (*see p.39*), and views from Golden Gate Bridge (*see p.8*) and Coit Tower (*see p.6*).

Have coffee at Vesuvio's (see p.45), buy a picnic at Molinari's (see p.22) to eat in Washington Sq Park, or browse in City Lights, owned by Lawrence Ferlinghetti (see p.18).

Palace of Fine Arts & Exploratorium ● 1E

A wistful, fairytale folly rising from a still lagoon, the Palace of Fine Arts is one of SF's treasured landmarks. Made in plaster for the 1915 Panama-Pacific Exposition, it was spared the wrecker's ball by tender-hearted San Franciscans and made permanent in concrete. Since 1969 it has housed the wonderful Exploratorium, a riveting science museum with hands-on displays on every facet of human perception – from the physiology of sight to the Tactile Dome, a pitch-black sculpture that visitors crawl, climb, and slither through (book in advance). *Adm. Open 10am-5pm Tue-Sun. 3601 Lyon St at Marina Blvd, T: 415 397 5673, www.exploratorium.edu*

The Presidio ● 2c-2D

Big and boundless, the Presidio is an awesome expanse of untamed marsh, dune, coast, and pine-woods stretching over 1,500 acres. It was a Spanish outpost in 1776, a Mexican fort in 1822, and then owned by the US army from 1846. The mammoth military base was closed in 1994 and turned into a national park: highlights include Baker Beach, which is the prettiest beach in the city, with wonderful views of the Golden Gate Bridge (see p.8), Marin County, and Crissy Field Park, a reclaimed shoreline park and promenade reaching all the way to

The Palace of Fine Arts

Fort Point National Historic Site (**1** 1C), a brick fortress at the base of Golden Gate Bridge (and the spot where Kim Novak feigned her suicide in Alfred Hitchcock's film *Vertigo*). T: 415 561 7690, www.crissyfield.org

SFMoMA **2** 6E

An electrifying, pared-down building by Swiss architect Mario Botta makes

The imposing façade of SFMoMA

The spire of the Transamerica Pyramid

a suitably theatrical backdrop for seminal work by Philip Guston, Eva Hesse, Ellsworth Kelly, Anselm Kiefer, Richard Diebenkorn, and Andy Warhol – highlights of one of the most vibrant modern-art collections in the world. Abstract Expressionism, Fauvism, Surrealism, Mexican Modernism, photography, architecture, and digital art all feature strongly – as does the shrine-like Museum Shop (*see box, p.20*), a luscious lexicon of contemporary

taste, from 'Bauhaus' caviar bowls to stools by Philippe Starck. For half-price admission, join the throng of art lovers on Thursday nights. *Open daily. Adm. Free 1st Tue of month. 151 3rd St btwn Mission & Howard, T: 415 357 4000, www.sfmoma.org*

Transamerica Pyramid **3** 4F

San Franciscans have grown fond of this pencil-thin pyramid, designed by Los Angeles-based architect William Pereira in 1972 and now an icon of the city. Piercing 853 ft (260 m) into the heavens, the 48-story quartz-coated scraper is set on concrete rollers that are designed to rock gently in an earthquake. (Literary

Siren Songs
At the far end of the Marina's harbor jetty (**1** 1E), the ocean waves make eerie music as they ebb and flow through Peter Richards' *Wave Organ*, an underwater sculpture constructed out of 25 plastic and concrete pipes in 1986.

Stairways to Heaven

A network of 400 narrow streets and stairways runs up and over San Francisco's steepest hills at angles of 45° or more. Two of the most beautiful and breathtaking are Telegraph Hill's Filbert Steps (*see above*, ❷ 3F), full of vistas framed by roses, ferns, and bougainvillea, and Russian Hill's Macondray Lane (❷ 3D), off Green St bet Taylor & Jones), a boardwalk street for walkers only, famed as Barbary Lane in Armistead Maupin's *Tales of the City*.

San Francisco associates the building with Montgomery Block, a 19th-century writer's hub with a saloon bar run by the real-life Tom Sawyer.) On Friday, don't miss the free lunchtime jazz concerts held in the adjoining redwood grove.
600 Montgomery St at Clay St, www.sfjazz.com

Yerba Buena Gardens & YBCA ❷ 6E

A great place to relax after a troop round SFMoMA, these beautiful

Yerba Buena Gardens in the sunshine

rooftop gardens are the ultimate urban Eden – a series of green and leafy rooms, with a 20- x 50-ft (6- x 15-m) waterfall memorial to Martin Luther King Jr, pools and fountains, butterfly and flower gardens, intimate performance areas, and two terraced cafés. Next to them is the dynamic Yerba Buena Center for the Arts, a challenging art museum focusing on new and diverse work and artists (*see p.29*). Open daily. Adm. Free 1st Tue of month. *701 Mission St at 3rd, T: 415 978 2787,*

san francisco places to shop

In San Francisco, the unique, the diverse, and the downright weird are cherished and revered as nowhere else. Whether it's pulp fiction or poetry, jeans that fit or custom-made corsets, 1950s' dinnerware or retro furniture, consignment cast-offs or designer fashion, candy or luscious deli delights, San Francisco can satisfy your every craving. For the spree of sprees, start your day in the style temples and department store palazzi of Union Square, then plunge headlong into downtown neighborhoods where you can stroll, browse, and linger to your heart's delight...

buy it places to shop

Top Shopping Strips

Castro ❶ 4E-4F

At the heart of the gay metropolis, Castro and Market Sts are a mecca for gifts and houseware, jewelry, gourmet food, and designer clothes ranging from elegant suits to ultra-trendy vintage, club, and streetwear.

Busy streets in Chinatown

Chinatown ❷ 4E-5E

Grant Ave is the main drag for trinkets, kitschy souvenirs, and knick-knacks, embroidered slippers, dresses, and antique chinoiserie.

Haight-Ashbury ❶ 4D

Vintage clothing paradise – plus all kinds of alternative stores from shoes, accessories, record shops, tattoos, and piercings.

Hayes Valley ❶ 3F

Crammed into three blocks between Franklin & Laguna, Hayes St is one of SF's ritziest shopping hoods: shop till

Summer of Love continues in Haight-Ashbury

you drop for chi-chi antiques, nifty shoes, and natty designer fashion.

Marina ❶ 1E-2E

Union St, Chestnut St, and Fillmore form a golden triangle of snobbish style-temples, from expensive but hip designer boutiques to yuppie chain stores, florists, juice bars, grocers, and giftshops.

The Mission ❶ 4F
Hit the Mission's ultra-hip Valencia St for salvaged furniture and thrift shops, designer-recycled clothes, Mexican folk art, secondhand and specialty bookstores and weird and wacky gifts.

North Beach ❷ 3E
With its funky New York NoLita-style boutiques and quirky stores, hidden-away Upper Grant Ave is one of SF's very coolest shopping hotspots.

Pacific Heights ❷ 4A
Elegant, expensive, and ultra exclusive, the Pacific Heights shopping enclave round Fillmore St is packed with upscale designer clothes, antiques, and classic household goods.

Polk Gulch ❷ 5C
Polk St between Geary and Clay harbors a nexus of swish design and quirky antique shops.

SoMa ❷ 6F
Discount designerwear and sleek home-furnishings, especially around South Park, heart of SF's Multimedia Gulch.

Union Square ❷ 6E
The front line for San Francisco's most glamorous designer flagships, specialty stores and mega department stores. Nearby Maiden

Cosmopolitan Haight-Ashbury

Lane is famous for its upmarket one-off boutiques and art galleries.

Antiques

The Butler & the Chef ❶ 4G
French design classics and grandiose architectural ephemera: from zinc-topped bars to art nouveau doors. *290 Utah Street at 16th Street, T: 415 626 9600, www.thebutlerandthechef.com*

Dishes Delmar ❶ 4E
Kitsch 'n' classic 1930s-60s American dinnerware, from heavyweight Fiesta and pastel Lu-Ray to 50s space-age Starburst. By appointment only. *Haight-Ashbury, T: 415 558 8882, www.dishesdelmar.com*

Bookstores

Acorn Books ❷ 6C
Rare books of all types. If it's ever been published then you'll probably find it here. *1436 Polk St, btwn Pine and California, T: 415 563 1736, www.acornbooks.com*

City Lights Bookstore ❷ 4E
The legendary literary beacon, founded by poet and book evangelist Lawrence Ferlinghetti in 1953. *261 Columbus Avenue btwn Broadway & Pacific Avenue, T: 415 362 8193, www.citylights.com*

A Different Light ❶ 4E
Legendary gay, lesbian, and transgender omnibus. *489 Castro Street btwn 17th & 18th, Castro, T: 415 431 0891, www.adlbooks.com*

Get Lost ❶ 4F
Crammed with two floors of travel books, maps, and gear covering all parts of the globe. *1825 Market St at Guerrero, T: 415 437 0529, www.getlostbooks.com*

Green Apple Books ❶ 3D
Truckloads of books spreading over three storefronts: new and used, with listening stations for the excellent CD selection. *506 Clement St at 6th Avenue, T: 415 387 2272, www.greenapplebooks.com*

Kayo ❻ 6C
Thousands upon thousands of 1940s-70s vintage pulp fiction and magazines. *814 Post St btwn Hyde & Leavenworth, T: 415 749 0554, www.kayobooks.com*

William Stout ❷ 4E
Exquisite architecture, furniture, and design books, with a mail-order facility and 14,000 titles available. *804 Montgomery St btwn Jackson & Pacific Ave, T: 415 391 6757, www.stoutbooks.com*

Candy Stores

Ghirardelli Chocolate & Soda Fountain ❷ 2C
The famous spot where the chocolate was originally

> **Tax Facts**
> A local sales tax of 8.5 per cent is added on to purchases at the till – you can avoid paying tax if you're from out of state and can arrange shipment of goods by US mail.

Enticing treats at See's Candies

manufactured: served hot or melting over mammoth ice-cream sundaes, with a mini chocolate factory at the back of the shop. *900 North Point St, Ghirardelli Square, T: 415 474 3938, www.ghirardelli.com*

See's Candies ❷ 5F
Dating back to 1920s Pasadena and still providing California's daily peanut brittle, nougat, cream, and candy fix. *3 Embarcadero Center, Ground floor, T: 415 391 1622, www.sees.com*

Department Stores

Gump's ❷ 6E

Established in 1861 and specializing in expensive exotica: rattan sofas, silk chandeliers, a new jewelry section, Russian bed linen, ottomans, chinoiserie, porcelain, and pearls, all watched over by an 18th-century Ch'ing dynasty gold-leaf Buddha. *135 Post St at Grant Avenue, T: 415 982 1616, www.gumps.com*

Macy's Union Square ❷ 6E

A colossal space, with an eighth-floor Cheesecake Factory serving 34 varieties of cheesecake plus separate annexes for men (across the street) and home furnishings (on Market St). *170 O'Farrell St btwn Powell & Stockton, T: 415 397 3333, www.macys.com*

Neiman Marcus ❷ 6E

From Armani to Versace, the A-V of fashion, in a glass-domed emporium with a rooftop restaurant overlooking Union Square. *150 Stockton Street at*

The entrance to Gump's

Geary, T: 415 362 3900, www.neimanmarcus.com

Nordstrom ❷ 6D

Offshoot of the civilised Seattle store – famed for its shoes. *865 Market St at 5th, T: 415 243 8500, www.nordstrom.com*

Saks Fifth Avenue ❷ 6E

Fifth Avenue glamor, from the big old cheeses to some younger and fresher designer labels. *384 Post St at Powell, T: 415 986 4300, www.saksfifthavenue.com*

Where's the party?

Hit San Francisco on any given day and chances are a local will invite you to a party, happening, be-in or hip hangout. If all you've got are business togs then head straight to Villains (❶ 4E) for a complete original or limited edition outfit. *1672 Haight St, btwn Clayton & Cole, T: 415 626 5939, www.villainssf.com*

Designer Boutiques

Diana Slavin ❷ 5E
This self-proclaimed 'haberdashers for women' combines elegance with color. Designs are inspired by traditional menswear, yet given a luxe and feminine touch. *3 Claude Lane, btwn Sutter & Bush, T: 415 677 9939, www.dianaslavin.com*

Museum Boutiques
San Francisco is home to some of the world's ritziest museum shops. Top highbrow haunts include SFMoMA (*see p.12*), with art books, furniture by Philippe Starck, mobiles, and paper cameras; the California Academy of Sciences (*see p.5*), a must for night-sky videos and whale replicas, and the Exploratorium (*see p.11*), with gadgets and gizmos galore such as build-your-own robots and flashing yo-yos.

MAC ❷ 7B
Combining edge with comfort, Modern Appealing Clothing has beaten Gap as the dedicated fashion master's mainstay. *387 Grove St at Gough, T: 415 863 3011, www.sfstation.com/mac-modern-appealing-clothing-b130*

Minnie Wilde (off map at ❶ 4F)
Affordable, sassy clothes created especially for the modern woman by local designers. *3266 21st St btwn Valencia & Lexington, T: 415 642 9453 (WILD), www.minniewilde.com*

Saks Fifth Avenue brings glamor to town

Designer Discount

GoodByes ❶ 2D
Designer must-haves as worn by San Franciscan socialites and fashionistas. *3483 Sacramento St btwn Laurel & Walnut, T: 415 674 0151.*

Jeremy's ❶ 3H
Consignment cast-offs at massive discounts: Armani, Dolce, Westwood, Chanel, and so on. *2 South Park at 2nd, T: 415 882 4929, www.jeremys.com*

Folk Art

Casa Bonampak (off map at ● 4F)
Fair-trade Latin-American fare: Zapatista dolls, Mexican candy in banana, strawberry, grape, and spicy tamarind flavors, plus 'Day of the Dead' figures clutching cell phones and surfboards. *3331 24th St btwn Mission & Bartlett, T: 415 642 4079, www.casabonampak.com*

Polanco ● 3F
Mexican religious and folk art from the 17th century to now. *393 Hayes St at Gough, T: 415 252 5753.*

Sam Bo ❷ 4E
In Chinatown: Buddhist and Taoist banners, shrines, candles, incense, scrolls, paper prayers, and Buddhas. *51 Ross Alley, off Washington St btwn Stockton & Powell, T: 415 397 2998.*

Tibet Shop (off map at ● 4E)
A Castro landmark since the 1970s – Tibetan clothes, jewelry, peacock fans, and golden statues. *4100 19th St at Castro, T: 415 982 0326.*

Piles of cheese at 24th St Cheese Company

Food & Wine

Bakeries

North Beach has some of the greatest bakeries in the world – for melt-in-the-mouth heaven-sent joy, check out the heavenly cookies at Danilo (❷ 3E), *516 Green St, T: 415 989 1806,* the cakes and cannoli at Victoria Pastry (❷ 3E), *1362 Stockton St, T: 415 781 2015,* and the focaccia in Liguria (❷ 3E), *1700 Stockton St, btwn Greenwich & Lombard, T: 415 421 3786.*

24th St Cheese Company (off map)
More than 300 varieties of cheeses and samples galore. Fondue and raclette sets, plus a luscious array of gourmet food. *3893 24th St at Sanchez, T: 415 821 6658.*

Cake Gallery ● 4G
Among the traditional birthday bears and sentimental flowery offerings you will find some very strange cakes. *290 9th St at Folsom, T: 415 861 2253, www.thecakegallerysf.com*

Molinari Deli ❷ 4E
North Beach foodie nirvana: custom-made sandwiches and tasty al fresco delights. Make up a picnic and eat it in Washington Sq Park. *373 Columbus Ave at Vallejo, T: 415 421 2337, www.molinarideli.com*

Plumpjack Wines ❷ 3A
This place features a wide, choice selection of California's finest red and sparkling wines (*see p.39*). *3201 Fillmore St btwn Greenwich & Lombard, T: 415 346 9870.*

Ten Ren Tea Co ❷ 4E

Explore the ancient art of Chinese tea at this well-known tea manufacturer. Discover the delights of organic, flavored, and blended teas, including bubble tea made with tapioca balls in peanut, bean, and fruit flavors. *949 Grant Avenue btwn Washington & Jackson Sts, T: 415 362 0656, www.tenren.com*

Make up a picnic at Molinari Deli

Spas & Beauty

Sephora ❷ 6E

Every brand of cosmetic known to woman in a shrine-like shop where testing, touching, and trying out is encouraged. Has a home shopping facility. *33 Powell Street at Market, T: 415 362 9360, www.sephora.com*

Specialty

Alabaster ❷ 7A

For the exotic, the beautiful and the just plain weird, then pick up a gift at Alabaster. *597 Hayes St at Laguna, T: 415 558 0482, www.alabastersf.com*

Martin Dollard ❶ 2D

For the pampered pooch: Burberry macintoshes, sweaters, gourmet dog treats, loungers, and Halloween costumes. *3429 Sacramento St at Locust, T: 415 643 7708.*

Paxton Gate (off map at ❶ 4F)

San Francisco's mesmerizing cabinet of curiosities features all manor of

Stuffed crocodile at Paxton Gate

unusual items, from mounted butterflies and beetles to stuffed animals (scary crocodiles) and bone jewelry. *824 Valencia St at 20th St, Mission, T: 415 824 1872, www.paxton-gate.com*

Swallowtail ❷ 3C

A nice line in medical paraphernalia – anatomical diagrams, palm-reading hands, and a bowl of artificial eyes. *2217 Polk St btwn Vallejo & Green Sts, T: 415 567 1555.*

Vintage Clothes

American Rag ❷ 5B

Designer-chic new and salvaged clothing from such famous labels as Stussy, Diesel, Donna Karan, and Spy. *1305 Van Ness Ave, btwn Bush & Sutter, T: 415 474 5214, www.sfstation.com*

Goodwill Industries ❶ 3F

Every item marked at $1.25, with new consignments arriving by the hour. *Closes at 3.30pm. 86 11th St at Market, T: 415 575 2197.*

Held Over ❶ 4E

Funky used clothing and secondhand T-shirt den featuring some very voyeuristic window displays (think prom-night restroom). *1543 Haight St at Ashbury, T: 415 864 0818.*

The farmers' market at Alemany

New Kid in Town

Ferry Building Marketplace ❷ 5G

Brand-new shopping mall on the Embarcadero, in one of SF's most famous historic landmarks, now all revamped and stuffed full of top-quality food stores. You will find restaurants such as the famous Vietnamese Slanted Door (*see p.40*), great cafés, and the Farmers' Market (*see box, p.23*) selling fresh foodstuffs. *Open daily. One Ferry Building, info@ferrybuildingmarketplace.com*

Go to Mark

Alemany Market

Wonderful Saturd market selling fres Dungeness crabs a locally grown and r exotica. An excellent flea market on Sundays. *100 Alemany Blvd btwn Crescent Ave & Putnam, T: 415 647 2043, www.sfgov.org/alemany*

Ferry Plaza Farmers' Market ❷ 5G

Farmers' market with luxury organic foodstuffs and stands of delicious produce run by local restaurateurs. *Open Tue, Thu, Sat-Sun. Embarcadero, www.ferryplazafarmersmarket.com*

Saturday on Stockton St ❷ 4E

Chinatown's amazing and truly kaleidoscopic fruit, vegetable, exotic fish, and shellfish market. Also a few items you might not recognize. *Stockton St btwn California & Broadway.*

san francisco entertainment

San Franciscans relish their rich and eclectic arts scene. Audiences are sophisticated, open-minded, and all-knowing, making the city a blistering testing-pad for a diverse spectrum of trad-to-rad productions. As elsewhere in SF, cross-fertilization is the name of the game: the usual boundaries overlap or intertwine; bars, restaurants, pubs, and clubs double up as happening venues for open mike and poetry slams or experimental film and theater. Get the scoop on the latest happenings from native San Franciscans or look for detailed listings at *www.sfstation*, the free weekly San Francisco Bay Guardian (*www.sfbg.com*), SF Weekly (*www.sfweekly*), or SF Chronicle's Sun Datebook (*www.sfgate.com*).

watch it entertainment

Arts & Theater

As well as robust classical theater and big-cheese Broadway hits, San Francisco makes room for some wildly offbeat fringe productions. For overviews, check the *Sunday Chronicle Datebook* and listings in the *Bay Guardian* and *SF Arts Monthly* (online at *www.sfarts.org*). Buy tickets at venues or online at *www.ticketweb.com*

Armageddon Outta Here

Far-out sculptor Mark Pauline and his Survival Research Lab stage roving demonstrations of his mad machines in public spaces throughout San Francisco – so far no spectators have actually been injured by the hazardous mix of explosions, fires, and screaming noises that make up the shows, but nevertheless spectators must sign waivers to attend, *www.srl.org*

Half-price TIX

The TIX Booth (**2**6E) at Union Square sells half-price same-day tickets for theater, dance, and music productions on the day of the performance. **Open 11am-6pm Tue-Thu, 11am-7pm Fri-Sat, 11am-3pm Sun. Powell St btwn Geary & Post, T: 415 433 7827 www.theatrebayarea.org**

American Conservatory Theater (ACT) **2** 6D

Contemporary and classical works, from Sam Shepherd and Charles Mee to blazingly innovative new writing. *Geary Theater, 415 Geary St at Taylor, T: 415 749 2228, www.act-sfbay.org*

Beach Blanket Babylon **2** 3E

The immortal San Francisco musical revue is an orgy of kitsch and camp, originally premièred in 1974. *Club Fugazi, 678 Green St btwn Columbus Ave & Powell, T: 415 421 4222, www.beachblanketbabylon.com*

Best of Broadway

Spectaculars in three rococo theaters. *T: 451 551 2000, www.bestofbroadway-sf.com*

Curran **2** 6D
445 Geary St btwn Mason & Taylor.

EXITheater **2** 6D
Hub of the SF Fringe Festival (Sept). *156 Eddy St btwn Mason & Taylor, T: 451 931 1094, www.sffringe.org*

Golden Gate **2** 7D
1 Taylor St btwn 6th & Market.

The Marsh (off map at **1** 4F)
High-quality avant-garde theatre. *1062 Valencia St at 22nd, T: 451 826 5750, www.themarsh.org*

Orpheum **2** 7C
1192 Market St at Hyde.

Project Artaud Theater **1** 4G
Pioneering arts complex in the Mission: performances and art spaces. *450 Florida St at 17th, T: 451 626 4370, www.artaud.org*

Looking across town from the YBCA

Arts Centers

San Francisco Public Library ❷ 7C
Poetry and book readings; free film screenings. *100 Larkin St at Grove, T: 415 557 4400, www.sfpl.org*

Yerba Buena Center for the Arts (YBCA) ❷ 6E
Vibrant downtown arts hub with a screening room, theater, galleries, discussion forum, and Internet café (*see p.13*). *701 Mission St at 3rd St, T: 451 978 2787, www.ybca.org*

Cinema & Movies

Film is revered in San Francisco, and the city is a buzzing film-festival haven for all kinds of independent, low-budget, and experimental arthouse productions. Check the *Chronicle* and *SF Bay Guardian* for listings or see *www.sfstation.com*.

Book ahead on the Moviefone, *T: 415 777 3456, www.movietickets.com*

Castro Theatre ❶ 4E
The Peter Pan of atmospheric movie palaces, dating from 1922 and with a splendidly ornate interior, classic flicks, and nightly live performances on the cinema's original Wurlitzer. *429 Castro St at Market, T: 415 621 6120, www.thecastrotheatre.com*

Wurlitzer in the Castro Theatre

Landmark Lumière ❷ 5C
This cinema screens films from foreign parts – mainly arthouse. *1572 California St btwn Polk & Larkin, T: 415 267 4893, www.landmarktheatres.com*

Red Vic Movie House ❶ 4D
Haight-Ashbury institution with sofas, wholesome snacks, and a chilled-out mix of quirky, cultish offerings. *1727 Haight St at Cole, T: 415 668 3994, www.redvicmoviehouse.com*

Sony Metreon IMAX ❷ 6E
15-screen multiplex mall, with a 600-seat IMAX. *1501 4th St at Mission, T: 415 537 3470, www.metreon.com*

Classical Music

A dynamic and diverse scene, ranging from classics to avant-garde, contemporary, early music, and opera. Standbys are available two hours before performances. Buy tickets from box offices, websites or TicketMaster, *T: 415 512 7770, www.ticketmaster.com*

San Francisco Opera ❷ 7B
Sumptuous productions featuring world-class opera singers. *War Memorial Opera House, 301 Van Ness Ave at Grove St, T: 415 864 3330, www.sfopera.com*

San Francisco Performances
Chamber music, instrumental recitals, 21st-century compositions, jazz and dance held in churches, at Yerba Buena (*see p.29*), and the Herbst Theater. *401 Van Ness Ave at McAllister, T: 415 621 6600, www.performances.org*

San Francisco Symphony ❷ 7B
American classics in the acoustically magnificent Louise M Davies Symphony Hall. Standing-room tickets sold from 10.30am on the day of performance. *Davies Symphony Hall, 201 Van Ness Ave at Grove St, T: 415 864 6000, www.sfsymphony.org*

Comedy

Lots of clubs, cafés, and other venues have open mikes for stand-up, slams,

and literary readings. To find out what's on, check the *Chronicle* or see the literary arts pages at *www.sfstation.com*

Brainwash ❶ 3G
This is one of the city's quirkier combinations – a bar, café, and laundromat with a disco, open mic, and poetry readings. *1122 Folsom St btwn 7th & 8th, T: 415 255 4866, www.brainwash.com*

Noontime Concerts
SF's excellent, free noontime concerts showcase anything from rhythmic Latin-American music to Mozart: venues include St Patrick's (❷ 6E), with its Tiffany stained-glass windows, *Wed 12.30pm, 756 Mission St, www.stpatricksf.org* and the Bank of America Center's Giannini Auditorium, (❷ 5E), *Tue 12.30pm, 555 California St at Kearny. T: 415 777 3211, www.noontimeconcerts.org*

The extravagant home of the San Francisco Opera and Ballet

Cobb's Comedy Club ② 2D
North Beach comedy institution. Very popular with locals and visitors alike. *915 Columbus Ave at Chestnut, T: 415 928 4320.*

Punchline ② 4F
Stand-up club with a bar, restaurant, and comedy from 9pm. *444 Battery St at Clay, T: 415 397 7573, www.punchlinecomedyclub.com*

Dance

San Francisco is home to ballet, modern dance, and dance theater companies all producing original work. Venues include YBCA (see p.29), Herbst Theater and Project Artaud Theater (see p.28). *www.baydance.com*

ODC ① 4G
Creates new works and hosts touring productions, also ethnic dance. *3153 17th St btwn S Van Ness Ave & Folsom, T: 415 863 9834, www.odcdance.org*

San Francisco Ballet ② 7B
The oldest ballet company in America: renowned for pushing classical dance to its limits. *War Memorial Opera House, 301 Van Ness Ave at Grove St, T: 415 861 5600, www.sfballet.org*

Jazz & Blues

Biscuits & Blues ② 6D
Quality mix of blues, soul, and Southern cuisine. *401 Mason St at Geary, Union Sq, T: 415 292 2583, www.biscuitsandblues.com*

Boom Boom Room ② 6A
Sultry blues bar showcasing a host of legends from Elvis Costello to its former artist-in-residence, the

> ### I'm Burning Up!
> In the city that spawned political activism, Crowded Fire acts as the leading theatrical light to inform and entertain its audiences. The company programs both premières and revivals of challenging works at venues scattered across the city. From formal theatres to open-air parking lots – anywhere and everywhere is a potential stage. *T: 415 675 5995, www.crowdedfire.org*

Wash your jeans, listen to poetry, or chew gum at Brainwash

legendary John Lee Hooker. *1601 Fillmore St at Geary, T: 415 673 8000, www.boomboomblues.com*

Elbo Room ❶ 4F

Jazz fusion and rockabilly with SF's longest happy hour (*5pm-9pm daily*). *647 Valencia St btwn 17th & 18th, T: 415 552 7788, www.elbo.com*

Nightclubs

Subterranean clubs and maverick mobile parties are on the rise in this city where almost anything goes. To find out what is going on, listen to

the grapevine, pick up freebie mags, or look for listings either in the newspapers or online at *www.sfstation.com*

The Endup ❶ 3G

Famous for its 6am Sunday T-Dance. *401 6th St at Harrison, T: 415 646 0999, www.theendup.com*

1015 Folsom ❶ 3G

Massive club with six dance floors, six bars, and DJ-centric danceteria events. *1015 Folsom St btwn 6th & 7th Sts, T: 415 431 1200, www.1015.com*

Mighty ❶ 4G

Named by *URB* magazine as the 'Best New Club in America' in 2005, Mighty is currently the hottest club in town. It's a great place to go to thanks to sleek interiors and an impressive sound system. *119 Utah St at 15th St, T: 415 626 7001, www.mighty119.com*

Milk's DJ Bar and Lounge ❶ 4D

R&B and hip hop are the name of the game at this friendly, modern venue boasting a large-ish dance floor. Guest DJs are known to pop in. *1840 Haight St, btwn Shrader & Stanyan, T: 415 387 6455, www.milksf.com*

111 Minna Gallery ❷ 6F

Art gallery, bar, and nightclub, hosting salon-style events. Dance floor for house and garage. *111 Minna St at 2nd, T: 415 974 1719, www.111minnagallery.com*

Sno-Drift ❶ 4H

Cheesy 1960s' ski-lodge/cocktail lounge with haute-Californian cuisine and VIP booths for hire. *1830 3rd St at 16th, T: 415 431 4766.*

Suite One8One ❷ 6D

This is San Francisco's most exclusive club. Endure the lines to blag your way into one of the VIP rooms to make your night extra special. 181 Eddy St at Taylor, T: 415 345 9900, www.suiteone8one.com

Rock & Pop

Bimbo's 365 Club ❷ 3D

Established in 1931 and still in the same family, this North Beach club and former speakeasy has hosted famous names from Blur to Macy Gray and Supergrass. 1025 Columbus Ave at Chestnut, T: 415 474 0365, www.bimbos365club.com

Bottom of the Hill ❶ 4G

From hard rock to rockabilly, post-punk funk and art-rock cabaret, with a happy hour, pool tables, and an outside patio. 1233 17th St at Missouri, T: 415 621 4455, www.bottomofthehill.com

Fillmore ❶ 3F

Bill Graham's rock and pop temple. 1805 Geary Blvd at Fillmore St, T: 415 346 6000, www.thefillmore.com

Great American Music Hall ❷ 6C

Elegant in Barbary Coast bordello-style, with bars, a stage, dance floor, and good acoustics. 859 O'Farrell St btwn Polk & Larkin, T: 415 885 0750, www.musichallsf.com

Slim's ❶ 4G

This is a great launchpad for touring rock and jazz bands. Especially good to catch new, up-and-coming bands as they are just starting out. 333 11th St btwn Folsom & Harrison, T: 415 255 0333, www.slims-sf.com

The Warfield ❷ 6D

Former 1920s music hall: now a hip and happening pop-palace with surround-sound acoustics. 982 Market St btwn 5th & 6th, T: 415 775 7722.

Inside the Great American Music Hall

Sound Sculpture

For culture vultures no visit to SF is complete without experiencing the awesome Audium, (❷ 5B), a pitch-black 49-seat theater where composer Stan Shaff and his collaborator Doug McEachern use 169 speakers to sculpt surreal compositions from synthesized and 'real' musical sounds. Performances Fridays & Saturday at 8.30pm.
Adm. 1616 Bush St at Franklin, T: 415 771 1616, www.audium.org

Sport

Ballooning

Above the Wine Country
Luxury ballooning over coasts, vineyards, redwoods, and geysers, with champagne brunch included.
2508 Burnside Rd, Sebastopol, T: 707 538 7359, www.balloontours.com

Baseball

The reigning supremos are the San Francisco Giants and their cross-town rivals the Oakland As. Tickets always sell out, but it's fairly easy to source them through *T: 650 227 3225, www.infieldadvantage.com*

Oakland A's ❹
McAfee Coliseum, T: 510 568 5600, www.oaklandathletics.com

San Francisco Giants at play

San Francisco Giants ❶ 3H
SBC Park, T: 415 972 2000, www.sfgiants.com

Basketball

Even with their modest successes, the Warriors command a loyal and passionate following.

Golden State Warriors ❹
Oakland Arena, T: 510 986 2200, www.warriors.com, www.nba.com/warriors

Beaches

The Pacific Ocean can be treacherous without a wetsuit, especially at Ocean Beach (❶ 4A), where powerful rip currents can sweep the strongest swimmers out to sea in an instant. The water is warmer (and cleaner) on Baker Beach (❶ 2B), with its panoramic views of Golden Gate Bridge and Marin County.

Biking, Riding, & Blading

Top haunts include Golden Gate Park (closed to autos on Sunday) and the

The Warriors have a huge following

Coastal Trail, a 4-mile (6.5-km) promenade linking Aquatic Park with Golden Gate Bridge (❶ 1F-1C) and Ocean Beach (❶ 4A). From Golden Gate Bridge, it is an 8-mile (13-km), two to four hour ride to Marin County. Return by ferry or continue 8 miles (13 km) to the sea at Tiburon or upwards to the 2,600-ft (792-m) summit of Mount Tamalpais (www.ridgetrail.org).

Blazing Saddles ❷ 2D

1095 Columbus at Francisco Street, T: 415 202 8888, www.blazingsaddles.com

Golden Gate Park Skates & Bikes ❶ 4C

Hire bikes, roller blades, and inline skates. *3038 Fulton St btwn 6th & 7th Aves, T: 415 668 1117.*

Skates on Haight ❶ 4D

Hire skateboards, inline skates, and snowboards. *1818 Haight St at Stanyan St, T: 415 752 8375, www.skatesonhaight.com*

Football

Unless you're royalty or prepared to shell out lots of money, getting hold of tickets to the Niners will be more or less impossible. Snagging tickets for the rowdy, beer-guzzling, hugely popular Oakland Raiders is easier (via the web site), though still tricky.

Oakland Raiders ❹

McAfee Coliseum, 7000 Coliseum Way, Oakland, T: 510 864 5000, www.raiders.com

San Francisco 49ers

Monster Park, Bayview, T: 415 656 4900, www.sf49ers.com

Golf

Lincoln Park Golf Course ❶ 3B

This course has great views of Golden Gate bridge as you play. *300 34th Ave & Clement St, T: 415 221 9911.*

Presidio Golf Course ❶ 2D

Open to the public. *300 Finley Rd, Presidio Park, T: 415 561 4653, www.presidiogolf.com*

Hockey

San Jose Sharks

The Sharks have a poor track record but a zealous fan-base; tickets to see them are tough to come by. *San Jose Area, 525 W Santa Clara St, T: 408 287 9200, www.sj-sharks.com*

Kayaking

Sea Trek Kayaks

Starlight paddles along the Sausalito waterfront with views of the city skyline: no experience needed. *Harbor Drive, T: 415 488 1000, www.seatrekkayak.com*

san francisco places to eat and drink

In San Francisco, food reflects the city psyche. Dishes from every corner of the globe are absorbed, cross-bred, and reinvented with a passion and attention to detail unparalleled anywhere else. Whether it's crab or mussels, noodles, burgers, or burritos, the freshest, highest-quality ingredients are wood-oven roasted, pan-seared, grilled, and lovingly cajoled onto a high plane of sophistication. Dining out in San Francisco is an event: for swanky restaurants book ahead, or opt for bar-food, theater menus, brunch, and breakfast options. For last-minute reservations, check out *www.opentable.com*. Otherwise take your pick from a galaxy of laidback neighborhood coffeehouses, bars, and restaurants in North Beach and the Mission.

taste it places to eat and drink

Price Guide
Prices based on a three-course meal without alcohol.
$ cheap (under $20)
$$ inexpensive ($20-30)
$$$ expensive ($30-50)
$$$$ very expensive ($50 +)

Breakfast

For brunch ideas, see box, p.39.

Powell's Place $ ❷ 6A
Authentic southern-fried chicken, catfish fried in cornmeal, corn muffins, and sweet potato pie. *1521 Eddy St (near Fillmore), Western Addition, T: 415 409 1388.*

Ritz-Carlton ❷ 5E
Poshest of the posh and a treat for Sunday. See box, p.39.

Zuni $$$ ❶ 3F
The quintessential weekend brunch – very stylish (see p.43). Open 11.30am-12 midnight Tue-Sat, 11am-11pm Sun. *1658 Market St at Rose St, Civic Center, T: 415 552 2522.*

Cheap Eats

Café Abir ❶ 3E
Combine fresh, organic goodies with a well-stocked newsstand at this friendly café that's busy throughout the day. *1300 Fulton St at Divisadero, T: 415 567 7654.*

Grind Café ❶ 4E
A Haight institution. Cure your hangover with one of the veggie omelettes or killer coffee brews. *783 Haight St at Scott, T: 415 864 0955.*

King of Thai Noodle House $ ❶ 3D, ❷ 6D
SF's favorite noodle chain: great-value noodle salads, soups, and stir-fries. **Branches:** 639 Clement St, T: 415 752 5198; 346 Clement St, T: 415 831 9953; 156 Powell St, T: 415 397 2199.

Restaurant Yo Yo $ ❶ 4F
Quality sushi in a groovy 50s diner setting. *3092 16th St & Valencia, Mission, T: 415 255 9181.*

Sam Wo $ ❷ 4E
Chinatown's ultra cheap 'n' greasy baptism by chow mein: bypass kitchen and machetes for noodles and steam rolls delivered by dumb waiter. *813 Washington St, Chinatown, T: 415 982 0596.*

Clam chowder in a bowl made of bread

Best Alfresco Brunch

For the dreamiest outdoor brunch, make a beeline to the Ritz-Carlton (**2** 5E) hotel's rooftop garden for the Sunday Jazz Brunch buffet – an epic feast of feasts involving champagne, caviar, blinis, omelets, sushi, smoked salmon, shrimps, carpaccio, cheese, baked goodies, fruit, and Caesar salad, all in for $70, or $35 for kids. *Open 10.30am-2pm Sun. Ritz-Carlton Terrace, 600 Stockton St, Nob Hill, T: 415 773 6198.*

Classic American Dining

Alfred's Steakhouse $$$$ **2** 4E

Steak-lover's paradise: banquettes, Caesar salad made tableside, and a whopping 32-oz porterhouse steak. *659 Merchant St btwn Kearny & Montgomery, Financial District, T: 415 781 7058, www.alfredssteakhouse.com*

Chez Panisse $$$$ **4**

The food-connoisseur's epiphany and the ultimate in Californian cuisine, founded by Alice Waters in Berkeley in 1971 and combining the freshest seasonal ingredients with the best Californian wines. *1517 Shattuck Ave btwn Cedar & Vine, Berkeley, T: 510 548 5525, www.chezpanisse.com*

The Fly Trap $$ **2** 6F

A true taste of old-time San Francisco offering such delights as: calf's liver and bacon, onion soup, sauteéd sweetbreads, and hangtown fry (an oyster and bacon frittata dating from the Gold Rush days). *606 Folsom St btwn 2nd & Hawthorne, SoMa, T: 415 243 0580, www.flytraprestaurant.com*

Tadich Grill $$$ **2** 5F

SF's oldest restaurant, dating from 1849 and still serving the definitive cioppino, lobster thermidor, and seafood grill. *240 California St btwn Front & Battery Sts, Financial District, T: 415 391 1849.*

Fancy Ethnic

Kokkari Estiatorio $$$ **2** 4F

Sublime, traditional Greek food in an

Eat Upon a Cliff

Only Upstairs at Cliff House is currently open for dining in tobacco baron Adolph Sutro's 1909 cliff-top mansion (**1**3A). It is undergoing restoration but it is still open to the public. No advance bookings, à la carte only, but with stunning views of Ocean Beach and Seal Rock: *1090 Point Lobos Ave, at Great Highway, T: 415 386 3330, www.cliffhouse.com*

Mother of All Breads
Chewy, crusty, tangy, and delicious, sourdough was brought to San Francisco by a Frenchman named Isadore Boudin in 1849. The starter dough used nowadays to make as many as two million loaves a week is descended from Boudin's original 'mother dough', a unique, fog-loving microorganism dubbed *lactobacillus sanfrancisco*. See this bread made at *Boudin Bakery & Café, 160 Jefferson St, Fisherman's Wharf, T: 415 928 1849, www.boudinbakery.com*

imposing dining room with a huge dining-table and open fireplace. *200 Jackson St at Front, T: 415 981 0983, www.kokkari.com*

Nihon $$ ❶ 4G
This fresh sushi lounge puts its emphasis on style and design. Complement your dish with one of 120 whiskeys available. *1779 Folsom St at 14th St, T: 415 552 4400, www.nihon-sf.com*

Thep Phanom $ ❶ 4F
Book ahead to sample some of San Francisco's most exquisite Thai cooking – from the delicate salads to the signature *tom kha gai* – chicken soup delicately laced with tangy galangal, lime, and chile. *400 Waller St at Fillmore, T: 415 431 2526, www.thephanom.com*

The Slanted Door $$-$$$ ❷ 5G
Awesomely sophisticated Vietnamese food, from clay-pot chicken and 'shaking beef' to great desserts and wines. *Ferry Building, T: 415 861 8032, www.slanteddoor.com*

Spring rolls at Slanted Door

Late-Nite

Mel's Drive-In $ ❶ 1E
Celebrate 1950s drive-in nostalgia in a setting of American Graffiti-style decor, including formica and jukeboxes. The food pulls in a good crowd, too: shakes, burgers, eggs any style. There's even a celebrity bar cocktail list. *Open 24 hours Fri, Sat 6am-1am Sun-Wed, 6am-2am Thu. 2165 Lombard St btwn Steiner & Fillmore, T: 415 921 2867, www.melsdrive-in.com*

Neighborhood Scenes

2223 Restaurant $$ ❶ 4F

Raucous Castro bastion famed for creative American cooking, and a mecca for brunch, lunch, drunken supper, and handsome waiters. *2223 Market St btwn Noe & Sanchez, Castro, T: 415 431 0692, www.2223restaurant.com*

Azie $$$$ ❶ 3G

Pan-Asian cuisine, DJs, high fashion quotient and prices. *826 Folsom St btwn 4th & 5th, T: 415 538 0918, www.restaurantlulu.com*

Nighttime along Grant Avenue, Chinatown

FC Impala $$$ ❷ 4E

Mexican food gets a bad rap in San Francisco. This eatery has a mission to take it into the big leagues – and it succeeds admirably. Popular with North Shore residents in the know. *501 Broadway at Kearny, T: 415 982 5299, www.impalasf.com*

Fringale $$-$$$ ❶ 3H

Slang for 'I'm starving', the bustling, noisy Fringale specializes in rich, earthy, French-Basque bistro cooking accompanied by jazz. *570 4th St btwn Bryant & Brannan, T: 415 543 0573, www.fringalerestaurant.com*

L'Osteria del Forno $-$$ ❷ 3E

Tiny, typical, and eternal North Beach trattoria. *519 Columbus Ave btwn Union & Green, T: 415 982 1124, www.losteriadelforno.com*

Sodini's $$ ❷ 3E

You'll be seated elbow-to-elbow at this intimate and popular neighborhood Italian eatery. Constantly packed, you will have to wait for a table unless you go really early. *510 Green St at Grant, T: 415 291 0499.*

> ### Drinking & Smoking
> Alcohol is served from 6am-2am; last orders are between 1.15am-1.30am. Smoking in restaurants, and indeed any other public indoor spaces, is prohibited throughout the state of California.

North Beach Pizza

Tommaso's $ ❷ 4E

The perfect North Beach pizza, cooked in brick-ovens to a deliciously thin crust: previous disciples of this joint include Nicolas Cage and Francis Ford Coppola. *1042 Kearny St at Broadway, North Beach, T: 415 398 9696, tommasosnorthbeach.com*

Potsticker Palaces

Most of the highest quality Chinese restaurants are located outside the Chinatown area.

Hunan $ ❷ 4F
Excellent lunchtime hotspot for scorching Hunanese cuisine: signature dishes include deep-fried pie and chicken noodle salad in peanut sauce. *924 Sansome St btwn Broadway & Village, N Beach, T: 415 956 7727.*

Yank Sing $$ ❷ 5G
A ceaseless round of steam carts flowing over with SF's best dim sum. *Rincon Center, 101 Spear St btwn Mission & Howard, SoMa, T: 415 957 9300, www.yanksing.com*

Jellyfish lights at Farallon

Pre-Theater

Jardinière $$$$ ❷ 7B
Celebrity chef Traci des Jardin's snazzy and sophisticated French brasserie – the perfect pre-theater rendezvous for cocktails, jazz, and dazzling balcony dining. *300 Grove Street at Franklin, Civic Center, T: 415 861 5555, www.jardiniere.com*

Raw Bar, Seafood, & Fancy Fish

Farallon $$$$ ❷ 5D
One of SF's most eye-popping dining rooms, a suitably aquatic mix of jellyfish lights, seaweed pillars, and extravagant, lavishly cooked fish. *450 Post St btwn Mason & Powell, Union Sq, T: 415 956 6969, www.farallonrestaurant.com*

Pesce ❷ 4C
Simple, yet delicious. Unpretentious, yet highly recommended. *2227 Polk btwn Green & Vallejo, T: 415 928 8025.*

Spanking fresh Dungeness crab

Swan Oyster Depot $-$$ ❷ 5C
Don't miss this San Francisco institution, with its original marble counter for slurping oysters and tabasco and fresh-cracked Dungeness crab. *1517 Polk St btwn California & Sacramento, T: 415 673 1101.*

San Francisco Treats

Alioto's $$$ ❸
Alioto's started as a sidewalk seafood stand. That was over seven decades

ago. Today, it is one of San Francisco's most beloved restaurants. The views of the Bay are worth the cost of a meal alone. *8 Fisherman's Wharf at Taylor, T: 415 673 0183, www.aliotos.com*

Crustacean $$-$$$ ② 5C

Diners put on bibs to crack open SF's biggest Dungeness crabs. Out of season (July–Oct) the crabs are flown in from Alaska. *1475 Polk St at California, Nob Hill, T: 415 776 2722.*

Fleur de Lys $$$$ ② 5D

A sumptuous golden tent and an explosion of flowers make a suitably mind-dazzling backdrop for the luscious culinary creations inspired by top chef Hubert Keller's native Alsace. *777 Sutter St btwn Taylor & Jones, T: 415 673 7779, www.fleurdelyssf.com*

Zuni Café $$ ① 3F

One of SF's most glorious dining experiences: glamorous, energizing urban cuisine – oysters, champagne, Caesar salad, pizzetta, and wood-oven-roasted chicken (see p.38 for

brunch details). *1658 Market St at Rose St, Civic Center, T: 415 552 2522.*

Schnitzel

Schnitzelhaus $$ ① 4G

Impossibly German. Schnitzel, goulash, strudel, sausage, beer, and waiters in lederhosen-galore in an 'authentic' pine-clad Bavarian eatery in SoMa. *294 9th St at Folsom, T: 415 864 4038.*

Fishy dining at Crustacean

Supper Clubs

AsiaSF $$ ① 4G

The ultimate fusion: top-notch Cal-Asian cuisine served by Asian 'gender illusionist' waiters, dressed in drag and lip-synching to disco-fever classics. *201 9th St at Howard, SoMa, T: 415 255 2742, www.asiasf.com*

Julie's Supper Club $$$ ① 3G

Retro club-diner (in the SoMa house where Patty Hearst was held hostage in the 1970s): perfect for late-night dining, cocktails, and dependable ribeye steaks, juicy burgers, grilled ahi (fish), plus roasted breast of duckling. *1123 Folsom St at 7th, T: 415 861 0707, www.juliessupperclub.com*

Sushi

Blowfish Sushi to Die For $$ (off map at ① 4G)

Trendy disco restaurant with lots of videos, manga, and sushi (including a mildly tongue-numbing strain of the infamous killer tiger fugu). *2170 Bryant St at 20th St, Potrero Hill, T: 415 285 3848, www.blowfishsushi.com*

Ebisu $$ ❶ 4C

This is possibly San Francisco's best sushi joint, serving moist, juicy, and esthetically enchanting fayre. It's also well worth the long no-reservations wait. *1283 9th Ave btwn Lincoln Way and Irving, Inner Sunset, T: 415 566 1770, www.ebisusushi.com*

Fresh shellfish are a delicious treat in SF

True Brews

Since the relaunch of Anchor Steam Beer in the 60s, San Francisco has led the hoppy, malty, flavor-packing microbrewery revolution. All the breweries have tasty bar food and most do guided tours: shrines to check out include the SF Brewing Co., with its unbeatable $2.00-pints, the Thirsty Beer, famed for tasty tapas, and Gordon Biersch, serving German-style beers on a Bay-side deck. **San Francisco Brewing Co.** (❷ 4E), *155 Columbus Ave at Pacific*; **Thirsty Beer** (❷ 6E), *661 Howard St at Moscone*; **Gordon Biersch** (❷ 6H), *2 Harrison St & Embarcadero*.

Tapas

Cha Cha Cha $$ ❶ 4D

Intensely jolly, legendary Haight St institution – tasty Caribbean/Cajun tapas and gallons of sangría.

1801 Haight St at Shrader, Upper Haight, T: 415 386 5758.

Ramblas $$ ❶ 4F

Trendy tapas in sleek and stylish surroundings. *557 Valencia btwn 16th & 17th Sts, Mission, T: 415 565 0207, www.ramblastapas.com*

Taquería

La Taquería $ (off map at ❶ 4F)

Mission's best and chunkiest burritos. *2889 Mission St at 25th St, T: 415 285 7117.*

Burritos being made at La Taquería

Buena Vista Begorrah

The Buena Vista saloon near Ghirardelli Sq was the US launch-pad for Irish coffee, brought here from Dublin in 1952 by *San Francisco Chronicle* columnist Stanton Delaphane. Sit at the bar and watch the barman line 'em up. *2765 Hyde St, (❷2C), T: 415 474 5044.*

Bars

Harry Denton's
Starlight Room $-$$ ❷ 5E

21 floors up with views across the city, dancing until 2am, velvet booths, champagne, oysters, caviar, and chocolate martinis. *Sir Francis Drake Hotel, 450 Powell St btwn Post & Sutter, T: 415 395 8595.*

Tonga Room $$ ❷ 5D

Stupendous rainstorm-and-lightning shows, with musicians floating by on rafts, make this nutty Polynesian theme bar one of SF's supreme delights. *Fairmont Hotel, 950 Mason St at California, T: 415 772 5278, www.tongaroom.com*

Top of the Mark $$ ❷ 5D

At the top of Nob Hill: old-fashioned, civilized hotel bar with panoramic views across SF. *Mark Hopkins Hotel, 1 Nob Hill, T: 415 392 3434.*

2202 Oxygen Bar $ ❶ 4F

Relax and replenish with a dose of oxygen delivered by tube in a range of affirmative flavors including 'aphrodisiac' and 'euphoric'. Pets and minors welcome. *795 Valencia St at 19th, Mission, T: 415 255 2102, www.2202bar.com*

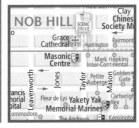

Coffeehouse Culture

The Beatnik id still lingers on in San Francisco's beloved North Beach cafés (❷4E), gritty hangouts of bohemian poets, jazz musicians, and artists since the 50s. Scenes to talk in, drink, play chess, and generally enjoy include Jack Kerouac and Allen Ginsberg's Vesuvio (*picture above*) and the family-run Trieste, where wait-staff stage opera sing-ins over caffè latte and cannoli on Saturday from 1pm. *Vesuvio, 255 Columbus Ave; Trieste, 601 Vallejo St, www.vesuvio.com*

san francisco practical information

Bounded on three sides by bay and ocean, and covering an action-packed terrain of 43 tall hills, plus beaches, valleys, dunes, and parkland, San Francisco is above all a city of neighborhoods. Roughly 40 principalities are packed into its 49 square miles (127 sq km), each with its own distinct personality, views, ethnicity, and culture. For those with sturdy calves, getting around on foot is a dream. Most neighborhoods are in easy walking distance and, when leg muscles begin to ache too much, there is always the option of a bus or streetcar. For epic rides on San Francisco's historic cable cars, expect to wait in line, or else turn up early in the morning or anytime from sunset onwards.

know it practical information

know it

Visitor Info

San Francisco Visitor Information Center ❷ 6D

Open 9am-5pm Mon-Fri, 9am-3pm Sat-Sun. 900 Market St at Hallidie Plaza, T: 415 391 2000, www.sfvisitor.org

Arriving by Air

With heightened security post 9/11, all passengers should bring photo-ID and allow a minimum of two hours check-in time for domestic flights or three hours for international departures.

San Francisco International (SFO) ❹

SF's massive international terminal: 15 miles (24 km) from the city centre; with two museums and an aquarium. It serves 50 airlines from an area the size of 35 football fields. *T: 650 821 8211, www.flysfo.com*

Oakland International (OAK) ❹

Small, efficient, and only 8 miles (13 km) from the city centre. *1 Airport Dr, T: 510 563 3300, www.flyoakland.com*

San Jose (SJC)

60 miles (96.5 km) away from SF but close to Silicon Valley. *1661 Airport Blvd, T: 408 501 7600, www.sjc.org*

Transport to & from the Airports

From SFO, cabs take 30-45 mins into the center: expect to pay $40 unless you're sharing. Cabs from OAK cost around $50, whereas cabs from SJC are a significantly more costly proposition. From SFO, Airporter buses pick up from ranks adjacent to

One of SF's fabled cable cars

the baggage claim areas every 30mins, dropping off at numerous downtown hotel locations for $10-$17, T: 415 202 0733. At all the airports, privately operated door-to-door shuttle vans pick up and drop off to multiple addresses every 10-15 mins ($10-17, available on a walk-up basis from designated ranks). A new BART (Bay Area Rapid Transit) train connection to SFO opened in late 2003: the station is located on Level Three of the International Terminal. From Oakland airport take an AirBART shuttle to Coliseum (15-30 mins), then a BART train into the city center.

Bay Area Rapid Transit (BART)
T: 510 817 1717, www.bart.gov

Mr Limo
T: 888 675 4665, www.mrlimo.com

Oakland Transport Hotline
T: 888 IFLY-OAK.

SFO Transport Hotline
T: 800 736 2008.

SuperShuttle Vans
(SFO & charter from SJC),
T: 415 558 8500,
www.supershuttle.com

Around Town

Buses, streetcars, and cable cars are operated by MUNI (the SF Municipal Railway): buy detailed route maps ($2.00) from newsstands and other retail outlets. T: 425 673 6864, www.sfmuni.com

By Bus

Slow but reliable, MUNI's orange-and-white buses are the easiest way to get around. Stops are marked by shelters, yellow poles, or markings on adjacent utilities; route numbers and names are displayed on fronts and sides of buses. Fares anywhere cost $1.50 and include a free 90-min transfer, valid for two additional boardings going in any direction. Have exact change at the ready (coins or paper) or use tokens (sold in rolls of 10 for $10.50).

By Cable Car

Restored in 1984 for $60 million, San Francisco's 125-year-old cable cars run on three routes, Powell-Hyde, Powell-Mason, and California. Manned by sunny-natured 'gripmen' (a San Francisco institution in themselves), the fleet of 44 cable cars departs at 10-min intervals from 6am-12.30am. The Powell lines are

Traveling by cable car

the most crowded and popular – especially Powell-Hyde with its hair-raising descent down Russian Hill to Bay St. Avoid lines by traveling in evenings or early morning, or board

Muni Passports
Available online or at shops, news stands, and other outlets, Muni Passport gives unlimited travel on metro, bus, and cable car for $11 (one day), $18 (three days), or $24 (seven days), plus discounts on museums and ferries, www.sfmuni.com

Hyde Street Turnaround

further up the route (stops are designated by pole signs showing cable cars). Fares are $5.00 one-way, www.sfcablecar.com

By Metro

Streetcars run below and above ground on six routes, including F-Market; fares are the same as on buses and stops are not announced en-route (*see downtown map*).

By Taxi

Medallion cabs are few and far between and nearly always full: San Franciscans mostly order them in advance, or cadge one off a kindly hotel doorman. Tips are 15 percent.

Veterans Taxicab Co
T: 415 552 1300.

Yellow Cab
*T: 415 626 2345,
www.yellowcabsf.com*

Take the Streetcars Named Desire
For the ultimate in streetcar rides, take one of MUNI's charming vintage 1930s F-market streetcars ($1.50) running up Market and Embarcadero (❷ 2H) to Fisherman's Wharf (❶ 2D-2E/ ❸), www.streetcar.org

By Train

The BART high-speed rail network is the quickest way to zip around the Bay. Eight stations in the city, such as Embarcadero (❷ 5G), Montgomery (❷ 6F), Powell (❷ 6E), and 16th St (❶ 4F) in the Mission, provide traffic-free links to Berkeley, Oakland, and Oakland airport (see day trips map). Fares are $1.25 within the city limits and $5 to the East Bay.

BART
*T: 415 989 2278,
www.bart.gov*

Bike, Motorbike, & Skate Hire

Even with steep hills and lots of traffic, San Franciscans are avid cyclists: a grid of marked-out cycle routes crosses the city and cycles can be taken free of charge on ferries, BART trains (outside rush hours) and on racks on MUNI buses. (*See Sports, pp.34-35*), www.transitinfo.org

EagleRider ❶ 4G

Harley-Davidson daily rentals and guided tours. *1060 Bryant St, T: 415 503 1900, www.hogrent.com*

Scootcar ❸

Scootcars – a combination of scooter, car, and tricycle – for hire. *431 Beach St btwn Jones & Taylor, T: 415 567 7994, www.scootcar.net*

Car Hire

With steep hills, stringent parking regulations, and constant gridlock, both driving and parking in San Francisco are a headache: if you do drive, remember to set the handbrake on hills and 'curb' the wheels. For trips out of town hire a car.

Avis

T: 415 885 5011, www.avis.com

Budget

T: 415 775 6607 or 800 527 0700, www.budget.com

Parking can prove problematic

Pay Less

T: 415 292 1000, www.paylesssanfrancisco.com

Changing Money

Banks

Hours are generally 9am-5pm Mon-Thu, 9am-6pm Fri. Most restaurants and stores take US$ traveler's checks and credit cards: ATMs give cash on Cirrus, Visa, and American Express cards.

Bay Views by Ferry

For $13, commuter ferries give great views of the Bay.

Blue & Gold Fleet ❷ 1D/ ❸

Fisherman's Wharf, Pier 41, T: 415 705 5555, www.blueandgoldfleet.com

Golden Gate ❷ 5G

Embarcadero Ferry Building, T: 415 455 2000, www.goldengateferry.org

Red & White Fleet ❷ 1D/ ❸

Fisherman's Wharf, Pier 43 1/2, T: 415 673 2900, www.redandwhite.com

Bureau de Change

Thomas Cook ❷ 6E
75 Geary St, T: 800 287 7362.

Climate

San Francisco has a steady climate; temperatures rarely vary more than 5-10 degrees either side of 60°F: July temperatures are 53°F-65°F max and December 47°F-57°F max (but it can get colder at night). In summer be

Sign for disabled access

ACCESSIBLE

Armed police officer on duty

prepared for daily fogs, in winter watch out for sudden downpours.

Cybercafés

Main Library ❶ 3G
100 Larkin St btwn 7th & 8th Sts, T: 415 557 4400.

Yerba Buena Center Café ❷ 6E
701 Mission St at 3rd St, T: 415 243 0930.

Yakety Yak ❷ 5D
679 Sutter St at Mason, T: 415 885 6908.

Earthquake Alert
For hourly updates, check the US Geological Survey web site at *http://quake.wr.usgs.gov*

Disabled Access

By law all public buildings must be accessible and have disabled toilets. Curbs are dropped at street corners; most buses can kneel, streetcar and train platforms are accessible by elevator. On Amtrak, guide dogs travel free and assistance is available. Disabled drivers with access placards can park free in designated blue-curbed bays. For more info, contact the Independent Living Resource Center, *649 Mission St, 3rd Floor, T: 415 543 6222, www.ilrcsf.org*

24-hour Drugstore

Walgreens ❶ 2E
3201 Divisadero St at Lombard (and other locations), T: 415 931 6417.

Emergencies

Police, Ambulance, & Fire
T: 911.

Access Health Care ❶ 4E
Walk-in clinic. *Davies Medical Center, 45 Castro St at Duboce Ave,*
T: 415 565 6000.

St Francis Memorial Hospital ❷ 5C
900 Hyde St btwn Bush & Pine,
T: 415 353 6000.

Left Luggage

Airport Travel Agency
Based at SFO International: large-size luggage storage, also shipping.
SFO International Terminal, Departures Boarding Area G,
T: 650 877 0422.

Lost & Found

Property Control (off map ❶ 4G)
850 Bryant St btwn 6th & 7th Sts,
T: 415 553 1377.

Streetcars, Buses, & Cable Cars
T: 415 923 6168.

Trains
T: 479 464 7090.

Mail

US letters cost 39¢ and postcards 24¢. Overseas letters and postcards cost 75-84¢. Stamps are sold in all hotels, vending machines, and ATMs on streets as well as post offices (open 9am-5pm).

Post office sign

General Post Office & Poste Restante ❷ 7C
Bring photo ID to pick up *poste-restante* mail: it is kept for 10 days.
101 Hyde St at Golden Gate Ave, Civic Center, T: 800 275 8777.

Public Holidays

Jan 1st	**New Year's Day**
3rd Mon Jan	**Martin Luther King Jr Day**
last Mon May	**Memorial Day**
Jul 4th	**Independence Day**
1st Mon Sep	**Labor Day**
2nd Mon Oct	**Columbus Day**
Nov 11th	**Veterans' Day**
4th Thu Nov	**Thanksgiving**
Dec 25th	**Christmas Day**

Telephones

Local calls from pay phones cost 35¢. For calls to another area, dial 1 + the area code. For international calls, dial 011 and the country code. Use credit cards, cash, or phone cards from stores, newsstands, and vending machines to make calls.

... of a Time

... ay-trip of a lifetime,
... Oceanic Society for
... ut to the Farallon
... ds in search of gray,
w... te, and blue whales, seals,
dolphins, and puffins; from
$50. Fort Mason Center,
(❷ 2B), T: 800 326 7491,
www.oceanic-society.org

Directory Assistance
411 (San Francisco).
1 + area code + 555 1212 (out of SF).

Call Collect
Dial 0 and ask to make a collect call.

Bison in Golden Gate Park

Cycle with the family around the city

Tours

Bike Tours

Bay Bicycle Bike Tours
Three hours across Golden Gate
Bridge to Sausalito (free bike hire;
return by ferry).
T: 415 346 2453,
www.baycitybike.com

Wheel Escapes
Tailormade guided bike tours for
groups or families; includes bike hire.
T: 415 586 2377,
www.blazingsaddles.com

Ferry Tours *See box, p51*

Food Tours

Local Tastes of the City Tours
Three-hour walking tour taking
in the best food shops, bakeries,
delis, and cafés in the North Beach
area. Tours of Chinatown and
evening culinary tours are also
available. *T: 415 665 0480,*
www.localtastesofthecitytours.com

Wok Wiz ❷ 4E
TV chef Shirley Fong-Torres's tour of
Chinatown's top tea-shops, temples,

shops, and herbalists, finishing with a seven-course dim sum lunch.
Wok Wiz Cooking Center, 654 Commercial St, T: 415 981 8989, www.wokwiz.com

Bus Tours

The Mexican Bus
Tour the Mission (see p.10) in a vintage Mexican bus.
T: 415 546 3747, www.mexicanbus.com

Tours in Strange Vehicles

Fire Engine Tours
75-min tours across the Golden Gate Bridge. *T: 415 333 7077, www.fireenginetours.com*

Gray Line Tours (cable cars)
From Union Sq to Fisherman's Wharf and the Bay area. *T: 415 434 8687, www.graylinesanfrancisco.com*

Duck Tours
Drive to China Basin and then plunge into the bay for a trip around Mission Rock. *T: 415 431 3825, www.bayquackers.com*

Walking Tours

City Guides
Free neighborhood tours organized by the public library.
T: 415 557 4266, www.sfcityguides.org

Cruisin' the Castro
Award-winning tours of Castro (see p.5), with brunch.
T: 415 255 1821, www.webcastro.com/castrotour

Walking through Golden Gate Park

And then Steam Clean
Unwind at the Kabuki Springs & Spa (**2** 6A), a bathhouse in Japantown with hot and cold plunge pools, steam room, and sauna. A day pass costs $15, or $55 with a 25-min Shiatsu massage, *Japan Center, 1750 Geary Blvd at Fillmore, T: 415 922 6000.*

Flower Power
Haight Ashbury (see p.9) and the Summer of Love. T: 415 863 1621.

Golden Gate Park
Free walking tours through the park, led by passionate volunteers.
T: 415 236 0991, www.frp.org

directory

For locals as well as newcomers, this San Francisco InsideOut directory has everything you need to get the best out of the city, from forthcoming exhibitions and annual events to finding the best hotels in all categories. There are suggestions for seeking out additional museums, galleries, and parks not included in earlier chapters. You'll also find ideas for further reading, listings of popular web sites, entertainment magazines, and local newspapers, as well as a special feature on how to speak the local patois like a native.

Places to Stay

San Francisco has more than 30,000 hotel rooms, ranging from vertigo-inducing peaks of perfection to summer-of-love crashpads. The swankiest places to stay are concentrated around Union Square and Nob Hill; for original European-style B&Bs focus on neighborhoods including the Mission, Haight, Castro, and North Beach.

Luxury Nabob

Campton Place $$$$ ❷ 5E

◤ ⫣ ⫙ ⩜ @ ≜ ❅ ℗

Well-heeled, stylishly understated, ultra-luxurious 'European' hotel on Union Sq. *340 Stockton St btwn Sutter & Post, T: 415 781 5555, www.camptonplace.com*

Key to Icons

Hotels		Museums	
◤ Room Service	@ Business Centre	⫠ Toilets	
⫣ Restaurant	≜ Health Centre	⧆ Disabled Facilities	
⫙ Fully Licensed Bar	❅ Air Conditioning	⌑ Refreshments	
⩜ En suite Bathroom	℗ Parking	▦ Free Admission	
		⚜ Guided Tours	

Price Guide

Price is for a double room.
$ budget (under $100)
$$ moderate ($100-$200)
$$$ expensive ($200-$350)
$$$$ luxury ($350+)

Huntington Hotel $$$-$$$$ ❷ 5D

Previous guests at this Nob Hill stratosphere of luxury have included Desmond Tutu, Robin Williams, and Princess Grace. *1075 California St at Taylor, T: 415 474 5400, www.huntingtonhotel.com*

Palace Hotel $$$$ ❷ 6F

Built in 1873, this hotel is considered the 'Grande Dame of the West'. After an extensive renovation, it is more beautiful than ever. The dining rooms, Garden Court ceiling dome and acres of stained glass will take your breath away. *2 New Montgomery St at Market, T: 415 512 1111, www.sfpalace.com*

The Ritz-Carlton $$$$ ❷ 5E

On Nob Hill, and SF's most up-market hotel by a clear margin: sumptuous 18th-century furnishings, award-winning rooftop restaurant, baronial beds *(see box, p.39)*. *600 Stockton St at California, T: 415 296 7465, www.ritzcarlton.com*

The Westin St Francis $$$$ ❷ 6D

Wonderfully old-fashioned hotel, home to the panelled Compass Rose Room – the venue for tea, cocktails, live jazz. *35 Powell St on Union Sq, T: 415 397 7000, www.westinsstfrancis.com*

Business Haven

Four Seasons $$$$ ❷ 6E

Super-swanky, business-oriented, in SoMa with a glamorous restaurant and city views. *757 Market btwn 3rd & 4th Sts, T: 415 633 3000, www.fourseasons.com*

Hotel Nikko $$$-$$$$ ❷ 6D

Serene Japanese minimalist luxury: tatami rooms, pool, sauna, and rock-garden. *222 Mason St at O'Farrell, T: 415 394 1111, www.nikkohotels.com*

Boho Hotels

Hotel Bohème $$ ❷ 3E

16-room Beat-boutique hotel in North Beach. *444 Columbus Ave btwn Vallejo & Green Sts, T: 415 433 9111, www.hotelboheme.com*

Hotel Diva $$$ ❷ 6D

The new-look Hotel Diva was unveiled in 2006 complete with

bespoke artwork, in-room iPods and an in-house soundtrack that uses the property as its influence. *440 Geary St btwn Mason & Taylor, T: 415 885 0200, www.hoteldiva.com*

The Phoenix $$ ❷ 6C

▧ ¶ ¥ ♨ 🏊 ❄ P

High-cool-quotient rock stars' pad with 50s motel decor and pool. *601 Eddy St at Larkin, T: 415 776 1380, www.thephoenixhotel.com*

Hotel Triton $$$ ❷ 5E

▧ ¶ ¥ ♨ @ 🏊 ❄ P

Highly trendy music-biz hotel with Dalí-inspired decor. *342 Grant Ave at Bush, T: 415 394 0500, www.hoteltriton.com*

Hot 'n' Hip

Clift Hotel $$$–$$$$ ❷ 6D

▧ ¶ ¥ ♨ @ 🏊 ❄ P

Another sparkler in the Ian Schrager diadem: surreal furniture. *495 Geary St at Taylor, T: 415 775 4700, www.clifthotel.com*

Hotel Monaco $$$ ❷ 6D

▧ ¶ ¥ ♨ @ 🏊 ❄ P

Cool take on a 19th-century grand hotel: marble staircases, fireplaces, and brasserie. *501 Geary St at Taylor, T: 415 292 0100, www.hotelmonaco.com*

Hotel Palomar $$–$$$ ❷ 6E

▧ ¶ ¥ ♨ @ 🏊 ❄ P

Luxurious, trendy hotel in lovely 1907 Old Navy store. *12 4th St at Market, T: 415 348 1111, www.hotelpalomar.com*

St Regis Hotel $$$–$$$$ ❷ 6E

❄ @ ♨ ¥ 🏊 P ¶ ▧

San Francisco's newest addition to the high-rise hotel scene. Good for visiting the buzzy SoMa arts community. *125 3rd St at Mission, T: 415 284 4000, www.stregis.com*

Value Hotels

Ansonia Abby Hotel $–$$ ❷ 6D

❄ 🏊 ♨ P ¶

Your grandmother would feel right at home in this quirky hotel that

feels like something out of an old Western movie. Come to think of it, you might like the cozy interiors too. *711 Post St btwn Leavenworth & Jones, T: 415 673 2670, www.ansoniahotel.com*

Commodore Hotel $$ ❷ 5D

▧ ¥ ♨ P

Designer hotel, home to trendy Red Room bar. *825 Sutter St btwn Jones & Leavenworth, T: 415 923 6800, www.thecommodorehotel.com*

Hotel Del Sol $$ ❷ 3A

▧ ♨ 🏊 ❄

Motel celebrating its 1950s Americana. Close to everything. *3100 Webster St at Greenwich, T: 415 921 5520, www.thehoteldelsol.com*

Golden Gate Hotel $ ❷ 5D

❄ 🏊 ♨ P

Dating back to 1913, this hotel maintains its Edwardian roots thanks to the interiors lovingly put together by the friendly owners. *775 Bush St btwn Powell & Mason, T: 415 392 3702, www.goldengatehotel.com*

Stanyan Park Hotel $$ ❶ 4D

Grand hotel decorated with lovely Victoriana. *750 Stanyan St at Waller, T: 415 751 1000, www.stanyanpark.com*

Budget

Grant Plaza $ ❷ 5E

Small, spotless rooms in the heart of Chinatown. *465 Grant Ave at Pine St, T: 415 434 3883, www.grantplaza.com*

Red Victorian B&B $-$$ ❶ 4D

Funky 18-room hippie crashpad B&B, peace-center, and gallery in the Haight. *1665 Haight St btwn Clayton & Cole, T: 415 864 1978, www.redvic.com*

Other Sights

Angel Island ❹

State park with hiking trails, tram tours, and a museum. *Open 8am-sunset daily. Take a Blue & Gold Fleet ferry from Pier 41 (❷1E/ ❸). www.angelisland.org*

Camera Obscura ❶ 3A

Architectural gem offering 360-degree views of the Pacific. *Adm. Open 11am-5pm daily. Cliff House, 1090 Point Lobos Ave, T: 415 750 0415, www.giantcamera.com*

Cartoon Art Museum ❷ 6E

Endowed by the late Charles Schultz. *Adm. Open 11am-5pm Tue-Sun. 655 Mission St btwn 3rd & New Montgomery, T: 415 227 8666, www.cartoonart.org*

Fire Museum ❶ 3E

Engines dating from 1810.

Open 1pm-4pm Thu-Sun. 655 Presidio Ave, T: 415 563 4630, www.sffiremuseum.org

Jewish Museum, San Francisco ❷ 5G

Explores Jewish identity: due to move to a new HQ in 2007. *121 Steuart St btwn Mission & Howard Sts, T: 415 344 8800, www.jmsf.org*

Maritime Museum ❷ 2C/ ❸

Delightful model ships, figureheads, and WPA murals on a fabulous Art Deco ocean liner. *Beach St at Polk, T: 415 561 6662, www.maritime.org*

Musée Mécanique ❸

Much-loved museum with more than 300 antique coin- operated fortune-telling machines, penny arcades, Wurlitzers, strength testers and photo booths. *Open 10am-7pm Mon-Fri, 10am-8pm Sat-Sun. Pier 45, Shed A at Taylor Street, Fisherman's Wharf, T: 415 346 2000, www.museemecanique.org*

directory

Museum of the City of San Francisco ❷ 7B

& ♦♦ 🖼

Small museum with the head of the Goddess of Liberty statue, which fell off City Hall in the 1906 quake. *City Hall, Van Ness Ave & Grove St, T: 415 225 9400, www.sfmuseum.org*

Museum of Craft & Folk Art ❷ 2B

& ♦♦

Crafts museum focusing on the very best in contemporary crafts. *51 Yerba Buena Lane, T: 415 227 4888, www.mocfa.org*

Tattoo Art Museum ❷ 3D

🖼

From photos to tattooing machines: next-door to tattoo-artist Lyle Tuttle's shop. *841 Columbus Ave at Lombard St, T: 415 775 4991*

Wells Fargo History Museum ❷ 5F

🖼

Gold Rush hoard: nuggets, gold dust. *Open 9am-5pm Mon-Fri. 420 Montgomery St, T: 415 396 2619, www.wellsfargohistory.com*

Annual Events

January

MacWorld Expo: decidedly techie, *T: 310 455 2886, www.macworldexpo.com*

February

Chinese New Year: *T: 415 982 3071, www.chineseparade.com*

March

St Patrick's Day Parade: Market St (❷7C-5G). *T: 415 345 4200.*

April

Cherry Blossom Festival (first two weekends): *T: 415 922 6776. www.nccbf.org*

May

Cinco de Mayor (1st Sun): Street party celebrating the Battle of Puebla. *T: 415 826 1401.*

Bay to Breakers (3rd Sun): SFers run 7.6 miles to Ocean Beach (❶ 4A). *www.baytobreakers.com*

Carnaval San Francisco (last week): steel drums and lots of dancing, *T: 415 920 0125, www.carnavalsf.com*

June

Haight St Fair (early Jun) (*see p.9*): Hippie fair, *T: 415 666 9952.*

Pride (4th weekend): Film festival and dazzling Castro (*see p.5*) parade, *T: 415 864 3733, www.sfpride.org*

July

Fourth of July: Fireworks, Fisherman's Wharf (*see p.7*), *www.pier39.com*

Marathon: *T: 415 284 9653.*

Cable Car Bell-Ringing Competition (end Jul): Fisherman's Wharf (*see p.7*), *T: 415 934 3900.*

August

Nihonmachi Street Fair (mid-Aug): Japantown's (❶ 2F-3F) lion dancers and taiko-drum street festival. *www.nihonmachistreetfair.org*

September

A la Carte, à la Park (Labor Day): Food fair in Golden Gate Park (*see p.8*). *T: 415 458 1988.*

Fringe Theater Festival (early Sept): More than 250 alternative theater performances. *www.sffringe.org*

Shakespeare Festival: free in Golden
Gate Park (see p.8).
T: 415 422 2222, www.sfshakes.org

Latino Fiesta (mid-Sep):
Latino Independence Day.
T: 415 826 1401,
www.latinbayarea.com

October

Castro St Fair (see p.5, early Oct):
T: 415 841 1824,
www.castrostreetfair.org

Jazz Festival (3rd & 4th weeks):
Big jazz names. T: 415 788 7353,
www.sfjazz.org

Exotic Erotic Ball & Halloween:
Masked ball in Cow Palace.
T: 415 826 1401.

November

Tree Lighting Ceremonies (late Nov):
Pier 39 (❷ 1E), Ghirardelli Square
(❷ 2C), and Embarcadero (❷ 5G).

December

Nutcracker:
America's oldest ballet co-presents
the Tchaikovsky classic at War
Memorial Building (see p.30),
T: 415 865 2000, www.sfballet.org

Listings

Find out where to go in SF for great
food, a film, or a wild night out:

San Francisco Chronicle

The city's Hearst-owned daily; has
Sunday Datebook covering arts and
entertainment.
www.sfgate.com

San Francisco Bay Guardian

Free weekly with excellent arts,
restaurants, and shopping coverage.
www.sfbg.com

SF Weekly

Rival free weekly, with equally in-
depth listings.
www.sfweekly.com

San Francisco Magazine

City-focused lifestyle magazine,
www.sanfran.com

Bay Area Reporter

Free gay weekly with listings.
www.ebar.com

Zagat

San Francisco restaurants: reliable
eating-out guide and listings.
www.zagat.com

Reading

*The Electric Kool-Aid Acid Test,
Tom Wolfe.* Way back in far-out
Haight: LSD parties.

*Stairway Walks in San Francisco,
Adah Bakalinsky.* 27 guided walks.

*The Maltese Falcon, Dashiell
Hammett.* Masterpiece of tangled-
web detective fiction.

Tales of the City, Armistead Maupin.
Funny, racy, gripping reading.

The Joy Luck Club, Amy Tan. Set in
Chinatown, explores the lives of four
first-generation Chinese-American
mothers.

Websites

www.fogwatch.com
Fog bank alerts.

www.sfgate.com/liveviews
Live views of the Golden Gate Bridge
from a webcam.

www.sfstation.com
Comprehensive SF listings magazine
online.

speak it

Since the Gold Rush of 1849, San Francisco has accommodated a vast and dazzling spectrum of dialects, languages, and argots.

In today's 21st-century San Francisco, the ethnic make-up is white (46%), followed by Chinese (32%), Hispanic (20%), African-American (10.5%), Filipino (4.5%), Japanese (1.6%), and American Indian (0.5%), leading to a colorful use of language and slang.

850 – 850 Bryant – the county jail in SoMa.

The Avenues – the Richmond and Sunset; residential districts with numbered avenues instead of streets.

B-Town – Berkeley, California.

Barbary Coast – nickname for Gold Rush-era SF, especially its bustling port and maritime district.

BART – Bay Area Rapid Transit, fully automated network of five high-speed rail lines linking SF with the East and South Bays.

Cioppino – traditional fish stew made with fish, crab, prawns, mussels, and clams.

Critical Mass – mass bike ride held last Friday of each month.

Dillos – short for 'armadillos', the heavily armored bike messengers zooming round downtown.

Dreltch – to temp in the Financial District.

Fillmoe or Moe – Fillmore District in San Francisco, also known as the Western Addition.

Fog Belt – the neighborhoods west of Twin Peaks.

Four fittaleeny – San Francisco county (a hip hop reference to the telephone area code).

The Gate – Golden Gate Bridge.

Geary Gray Mist – dense fog creeping over the Richmond.

Glass Ceiling – thin, persistent wisp of sun-obscuring fog.

God Blobs – fog-borne dew that forms in blobs on eucalyptus trees.

The Jungle – The Marin City housing projects where rapper Tupac Shakur used to live.

The Mish – The Mission.

Mobb music – Funk-based sound invented by producers Studio Ton and Mike Mosely, widely copied throughout the Bay Area.

Multimedia Gulch – SoMa neighborhood colonized by dotcommers in the 1990s.

Muni – San Francisco Municipal Railway: also its buses, etc. streetcars, cable cars and trolley buses.

The Niners – the San Francisco 49ers football team.

Oaktown – Oakland.

October Surprise – sudden, unseasonable blanket of fog.

The Rock – Alcatraz.

Sco – Short for San Francisco. Popularised by the rap community.

SoMa – the area South of Market Street.

Stanyan Shroud – damp, persistent fog extending right to the edge of Haight.

The Stick – Candlestick, in San Francisco, former home of the San Francisco 49ers and Giants.

Written by Vanessa Letts and
Ryan Levitt

Revision Management by
Cambridge Publishing
Management Ltd.

Pictures © Compass Maps
Ltd except John Heseltine
Picture Archive, Getty, John
Schoenfeld Photography,
The Exploratorium /Lily
Rodriguez; San Francisco
Convention & Visitors
Bureau (Sandor Balantoni,
Phil Coblentz, Rick Gerharter,
Jerry Lee Hayes, Jack
Hollingsworth, Sheryl
Schindler)

Cover Images: Getty/Jeremy
Woodhouse, Ulf Sjostedt

Whilst every effort has been
made to trace the photography copyright holders, we
apologise for any omissions.
We would be pleased to
insert appropriate credits in
any future editions.

info@popoutmaps.com
www.popout-travel.com
© 2007 Compass Maps Ltd.

Patents Pending Worldwide.
popout™cityguide as well as
individual integrated
components including
popout™map and
associated products are the
subject of Patents Pending
Worldwide

AA 3401

❸ FISHERMAN'S WHARF & PIER 39

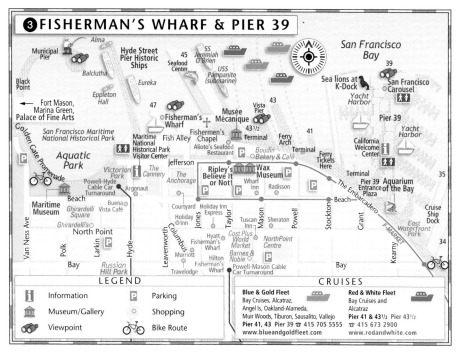

Municipal Pier
Alma
Black Point
Balclutha
Hyde Street Pier Historic Ships
Eureka
Eppleton Hall

45 Seafood Center
SS Jeremiah O'Brien
USS Pampanito (submarine)

San Francisco Bay

Sea lions at K-Dock
San Francisco Carousel
39
Yacht Harbor

← Fort Mason, Marina Green, Palace of Fine Arts

Golden Gate Promenade

San Francisco Maritime National Historical Park

Aquatic Park

47
Fisherman's Wharf
Musée Mécanique
Fishermen's Chapel

43
Vista Pier
43½ Terminal
41

Pier 39
Yacht Harbor
California Welcome Center

Maritime National Historical Park Visitor Center
Fish Alley
Alioto's Seafood Restaurant
Ferry Arch
Terminal
Ferry Tickets Here

35

Victorian Park
The Cannery
Jefferson
Boudin Bakery & Café

Powell-Hyde Cable Car Turnaround
The Anchorage
Ripley's Believe It or Not!
Wax Museum
Wharf Inn
Pier 39 Aquarium Entrance of the Bay Plaza

Maritime Museum
Beach
Buena Vista Café
Ghirardelli Square
Ghirardelli's
North Point
Argonaut
Courtyard
Holiday Inn
Holiday Inn Express
Radisson
Beach
The Embarcadero

Cruise Ship Dock
East Waterfront Park

Van Ness Ave
Polk
Larkin
Hyde
Russian Hill Park
Bay
Columbus
Leavenworth
Jones
Taylor
Mason
Powell
Stockton
Grant
Kearny
Bay

Hyatt Fisherman's Wharf
Marriott
Travelodge
Cost Plus World Market
Barnes & Noble
Fisherman's Wharf
Tuscan Inn
Sheraton
NorthPoint Centre
Hilton
Powell-Mason Cable Car Turnaround

F-MARKET

34

LEGEND

ℹ Information	🅿 Parking
🏛 Museum/Gallery	○ Shopping
🔭 Viewpoint	🚲 Bike Route

CRUISES

Blue & Gold Fleet
Bay Cruises, Alcatraz,
Angel Is, Oakland-Alameda,
Muir Woods, Tiburon, Sausalito, Vallejo
Pier 41, 43 ☎ 415 705 5555
www.blueandgoldfleet.com

Red & White Fleet
Bay Cruises and
Alcatraz
Pier 41 & 43½ Pier 43½
☎ 415 673 2900
www.redandwhite.com